The Creation Seri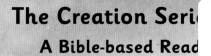

A Bible-based Read

Light, Sky, Land and Sea

Carole Leah
and Sharon Rentta

NOTE TO PARENTS AND TEACHERS

The Creation Series consists of eight books based on the Genesis account in the Bible. This is the second book of this series and has been written from a Christian viewpoint. It is intended to be read *to* 3-4 year olds. The whole series prepares children to read and extend their vocabulary. In this book children can develop and practise preparatory skills for reading as well as learn about the light of God's character.

BIBLE REFERENCES

All Bible references are in bold throughout and are as follows: p6: Genesis 1:3-4; p8: Genesis 1:4; p10: Genesis 1:6-7; p12: Genesis 1:9-10.

ENCOURAGE CHILDREN TO:

*   Talk about the illustrations and retell the story in their own words.
*   Find all the pictorial black stones and count them.
*   Learn the Bible verse and its reference (see page 24).
*   Look at the page numbers and count them in sequence.
*   Sort out their own toys into ones they can use in the air, ones they can use on land and ones they can use with water.
*   Ensure that the children know the meaning of these words: *calm* (still, not moving very much); *precious* (very special, hard to find); *separated* (pulled apart, put away); *space* (gap).

Carole Leah became a Christian at a youth camp when she was seventeen years old while reading a Gideon New Testament. She felt called to write these books so that young children would learn the truth about God while also developing their reading and vocabulary skills. Several people have worked alongside Carole as she wrote this material but she would like to especially dedicate these books to the memory of her dear friend Ruth Martin who gave so much support.

ISBN: 978-1-84550-530-1 Published by Christian Focus Publications, Geanies House, Fearn, Tain, Ross-shire, IV20 ITW, Scotland, U.K.
www.christianfocus.com

Todd, Joy and Daniel are with their dads and mums.
See what they are doing in this book!

Todd is with his dad and mum.
Joy and Daniel are with their dad and mum.

Can you find pictures of 8 black stones
in this book?

Did you know that some stones are precious?
They are found deep down in the earth.

In the beginning

God made the Earth round like a ball.

It was all dark.

It was covered in water.

The Spirit of God began to move.

He moved over the water.

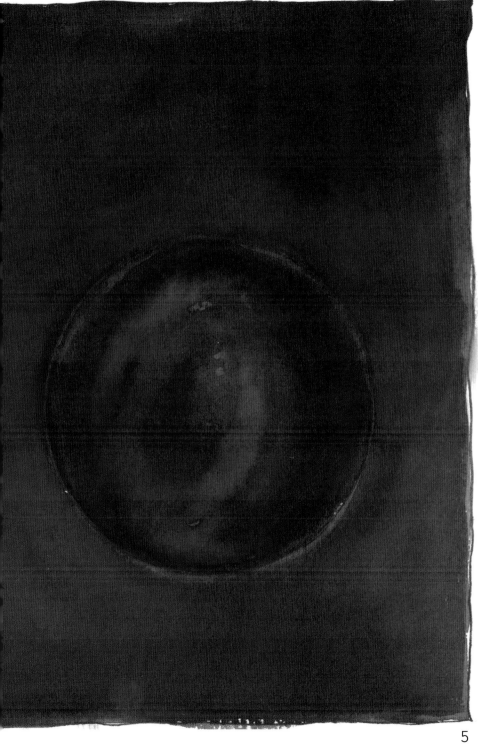

God said, '**...Let there be light...**' and there was light.

...God was pleased with what he saw...

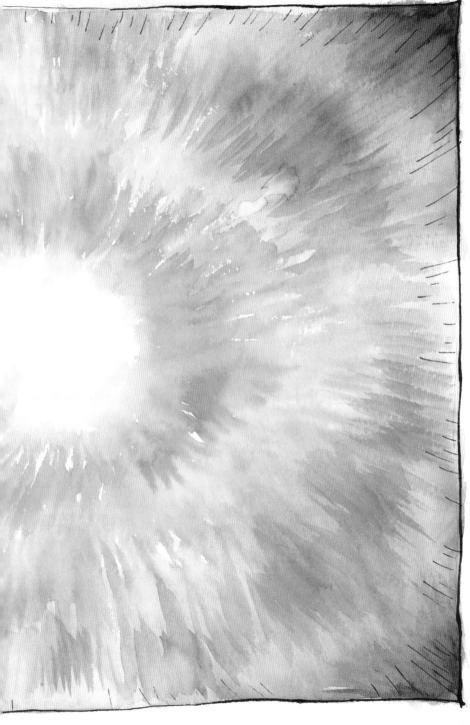

God ...**separated the light from the darkness.**

He called the light, day.

He called the darkness, night.

Then God said,

'Let there be a big space of air around the Earth.'

...It was done...

God called the big space of air, sky.

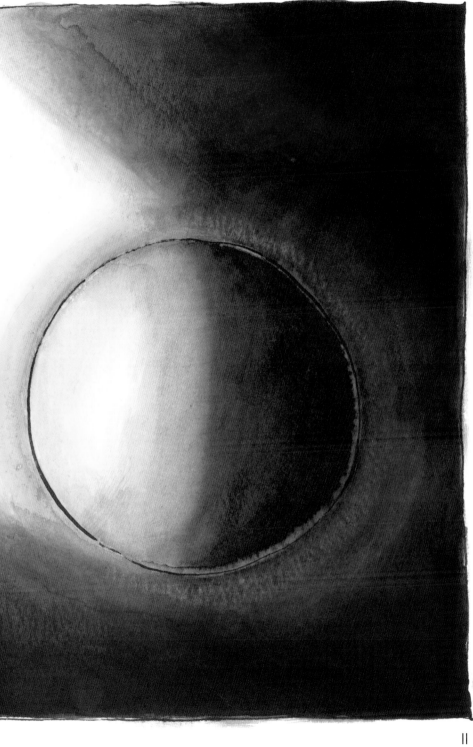

Then God said,

'Water, move into one place.'

...It was done, so there was dry land.

God called the dry land, Earth.

He called the water, sea.

...God was pleased with what he saw.

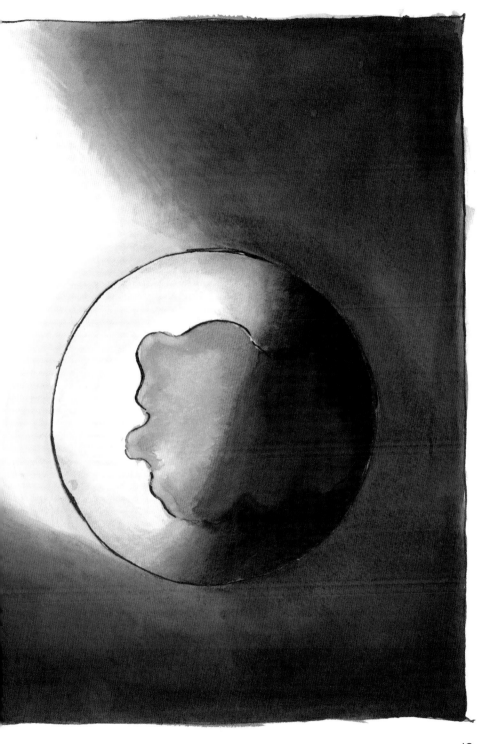

Now, the sky sometimes looks blue.

Sometimes it looks grey.

Sometimes it has white clouds in it.

Todd can even fly in the sky God made!

Now, some of the land is high.

Some of the land is low.

Daniel and Joy like to dig the earth.

They can find hard rocks and

interesting stones.

Now, the sea is sometimes rough.

Sometimes the sea is calm.

Todd, Joy and Daniel love to splash in

the waves of the sea.

Now, Todd, Joy and Daniel can see

everything in the daylight God made.

Joy and Daniel are happy.

Todd has come to stay with them.

They are all happy that

God made the daylight, sky, land and sea.

God is with them in the day and at night.

God is with them everywhere!

God is with us, too!

...God is light, and

there is no darkness at all in him.

I John chapter 1, verse 5